Tilly the Tooting Turkey

Written and Illustrated by
Drew Dally

ISBN: 978-1-959581-01-7

Visit our website to get more information and freebies
drewdallybooks@gmail.com

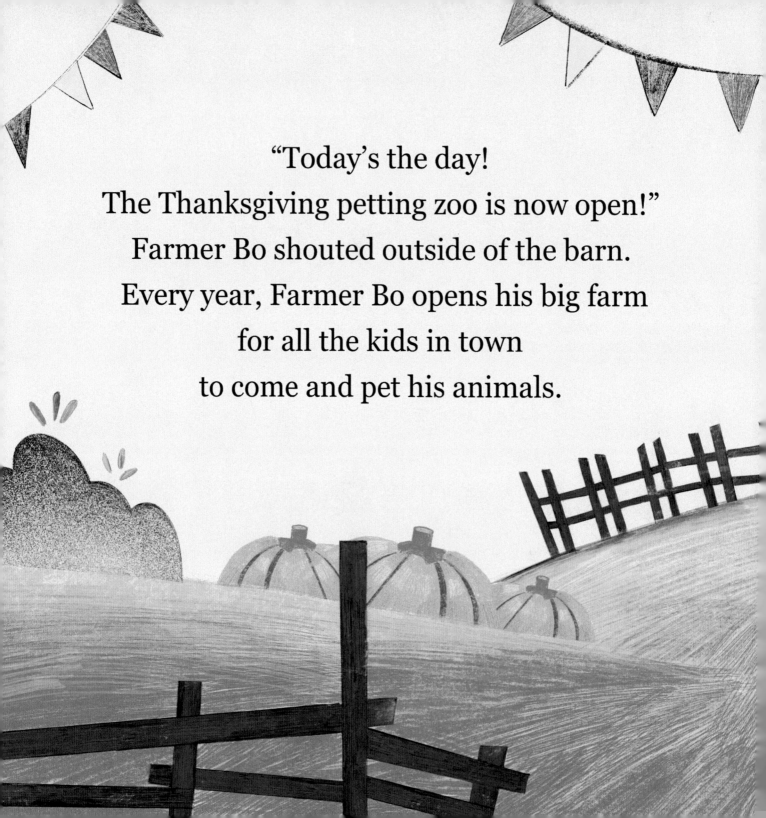

"Today's the day!
The Thanksgiving petting zoo is now open!"
Farmer Bo shouted outside of the barn.
Every year, Farmer Bo opens his big farm
for all the kids in town
to come and pet his animals.

He has cows, chickens, pigs, goats,
rabbits, and more!
Farmer Bo greets all his animals
and lets them out into their pens
while giving them yummy nuts.

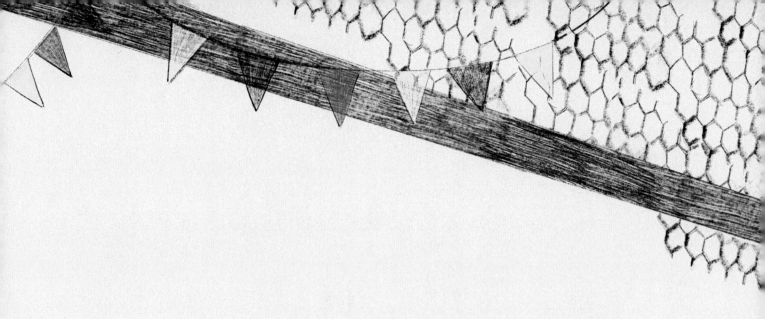

"This is delicious!"
Rocky Rooster says to Tilly the turkey.
"This is my favorite time of the year,
I love meeting the kids."
Out of all the animals, Tilly and Rocky
were probably the most thrilled.

The animals were led into their show pens
to get ready, when Tilly's tummy
made a gurgling sound. She looked down
and put a hand on her tummy,
"I don't feel so good, Rocky." She said with a frown.
"Oh no, what's wrong?" Rocky asked.
"I don't know, I think I have to-"
Just then, Tilly let out
the STINKIEST, LONGEST, TOOOOOT!

Tilly flew up into the air, flying side-to-side,
another wet TOOOT! "Woah!"
She yelled while zooming through.
The stinky toot was so powerful. It made her fly away!
Rocky fell to the ground, laughing!
"Ha-ha-ha-ha! You're tooting so much!"
Tilly flew down and laughed, "I didn't know
I could do that! That was so fun!"

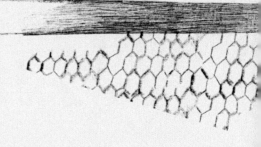

"Oh no, no, no! We can't have you tooting
when the kids arrive, Tilly!
You're going back into your pen; I'm sorry."
Farmer Bo saw what happened
and returned Tilly back to her pen.
"Nooo, please Farmer Bo, I won't do it anymore;
I promise! Please let me see the kids."
She begged him and pleaded,
but Farmer Bo shook his head
and closed the gate.

Tilly sat down on her hay nest and sighed.
This was the most horrible day ever!
All Tilly wanted was to see the kids
and now she must stay in here
and watch everyone have fun.
A second later,
'the same gurgling noise
occurred in her stomach.

Once again, another gross POOOT shot out
and made Tilly fly up in the air
and BONK! Her head on the ceiling.
"Ouch!" She flew all around yelling,
flapping her wings, trying to control her toot,
but it was no use!

She crashed into the barrel of nuts!
She groaned in pain, she wiggled
and squirmed her way out
and shook off her feathers.
"Now I see why Farmer Bo doesn't
want me in the zoo."
She said with her head down,
then a tiny pooot! Came from her.

"Awe, man!"

Suddenly, a laugh could be heard
from outside of her pen. She looked up,
and there stood a couple of kids giggling at Tilly!
Almost immediately, a bunch of kids stormed over
to watch Tilly,
"This turkey just farted so much;
she flew into the air!"
The kid said. "We want to see!"
The other kids chanted.

Farmer Bo was curious why everyone
was over at Tilly's pen.
"What's going on here?"
he said with his hands on his hips.
"The turkey tooted and flew around;
it was so hilarious!" One of the kids said.

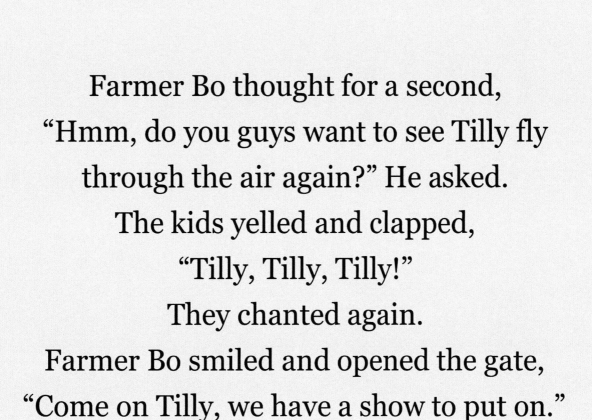

Farmer Bo thought for a second,
"Hmm, do you guys want to see Tilly fly
through the air again?" He asked.
The kids yelled and clapped,
"Tilly, Tilly, Tilly!"
They chanted again.
Farmer Bo smiled and opened the gate,
"Come on Tilly, we have a show to put on."

Tilly got up and zoomed to her pen,
where Farmer Bo started feeding her more nuts,
"Is that what makes her toot?"
One kid asked.
"Mhmm! Turkey's love nuts, berries, leaves,
insects, but Tilly loves nuts."

Farmer Bo gave nuts to the kids to feed Tilly,
and when she was getting ready to toot,
she backed up, "Here we gooo!"
She shouted and shot up into the air,
a wet TOOOT,
she let out and flew around in circles,
TOOOT, up and down,
TRUUUMP! Side-to-side, POOOF!

To o

The kids were laughing so much;
they only wanted to see Tilly toot.
"Again, again, again!"
They jumped and shouted with joy.
Tilly was having the best time,
making the kids laugh.
She was so delighted she could be
a part of the petting zoo this year.

Farmer Bo chuckled and smiled,
"Tilly loves tooting; that's why we call her
Tilly The Tooting Turkey."